# Foundations

# Foundations

*James Walsh*

Left Hand Books

The publisher wishes to thank the John W. and Clara C. Higgins Foundation for financial assistance granted as well as the Pauline Oliveros Foundation for their continued support.

**Left Hand Books website:** http://www.lefthandbooks.com/lhb

Credits:
Cover: "Foundation of Light-colored Stones." Photo copyright © 1997 by James Walsh.
Page 75: "House Foundation." Photo copyright © 1997 by Forrest Holzapfel. Used by permission.
Page 95: "Pathway to Infinity," from *Markings: Sacred Landscapes from the Air* by Marilyn Bridges (Aperture Foundation). Photo copyright © 1986 by Marilyn Bridges. Used by permission.
All other photographs copyright © 1997 by James Walsh except the photographs by Frank Iannotti of illustrations and text found in *Lake Dwellings*.

Designed by Bryan McHugh.

ISBN 1-880516-18-7

Manufactured in the United States of America.

# LIST OF WORKS

wall pieces:

Foundation
lead, brick, rubber mat
36 x 36 x 6"
1992

Foundation: East Kingston
brick, aluminum, tarpaper
24 x 24"
1993

Foundation: Malden
brick, aluminum, tarpaper
24 x 24"
1993

Foundation: Connelly
brick, aluminum, tarpaper
24 x 24"
1993

Foundation: Ulster Park
brick, aluminum, tarpaper
24 x 24"
1993

outdoor installations:

Foundation of Light-colored Stones
Rondout Creek, Rosendale, NY
10 x 20'
September 19, 1994

Foundation of Black Plastic Tubes
Eddyville, NY
6 x 12'
September 26, 1994

Foundation of Cattails
Eddyville, NY
10 x 20'
September 26, 1994

Foundation of Red Leaves
Marbletown, NY
18 x 36"
October 17, 1994

Foundation of Yellow Leaves
Marbletown, NY
18 x 36"
October 17, 1994

Foundation of Mason's Line I
Island Dock, Kingston, NY
10 x 20'
October 24, 1994

Foundation of Apple Branches
Ulster Park, NY
10 x 20'
November, 1994

Foundation of Flowerheads
The Commons, Kingston, NY
4 x 6 $^1/_2$'
December 12, 1994

Foundation of Sumac I
The Commons, Kingston, NY
4 x 6 $^1/_2$'
December 14, 1994

Foundation of Sumac II
The Commons, Kingston, NY
4 x 6 $^1/_2$'
December 14, 1994

Foundation of Seedpods on My Glove
The Commons, Kingston, NY
1 x 2"
December 14, 1994

Foundation of Mason's Line II
Kingston, NY
10 x 20'
December 28, 1994

Foundation of Trampled Mud
Kingston, NY
15 x 20'
December 29, 1994

Foundation of Bricks on Mud
Kingston, NY
24 x 36"
December 29, 1994

Barrytown Foundations
Center for Curatorial Studies
Bard College
Annandale, NY
dimensions variable
April, 1996

# Foundations

The 'boring' if seen as a discrete step in the development of the whole site has esthetic potential. It is an 'invisible whole,' and could be defined by Carl Andre's motto—'A thing is a hole in a thing it is not.' The 'boring,' like other 'earth works,' is becoming more and more important to artists. Pavements, holes, trenches, mounds, heaps, paths, ditches, roads, terraces, etc., all have esthetic potential. Robert Smithson, "Towards the Development of an Air Terminal Site"

All artistic structure is essentially polyphonic: it evolves not in a single line of thought but in several superimposed strands at once. Hence creativity requires a diffuse, scattered kind of attention that contradicts our normal logical habits of thinking. Anton Ehrenzweig, *The Hidden Order of Art*

I have always been attracted to foundations. For a year when I was young, from about three-and-a-half to four-and-a-half, we lived in an old house in East Brookfield, in western Massachusetts. The house had been built before the Revolutionary War by a man named Rice who, as I remember it, had participated in the Boston Tea Party. Some of my earliest memories are there, including one of standing at the edge of an old stone foundation. It was in a disused field overgrown with milkweed adjacent to our house, and it may have been a small house or more likely, a root cellar or other outbuilding. The walls were crumbling, with small trees growing up in the center. My memory is simply of being there alone, standing at the edge, looking down into the foundation.

My first artwork dealing with foundations, *Foundation* (1992), is a lead-covered, 36 x 36 x 6" box, in which is set a square of bricks two deep and two on a side. I had been producing a series of wall-hung sculptures from found materials—*Island, Quarry Pool, Marsh*—that were all abstracted, schematic landscapes seen in plan view, from overhead, simplifying the land forms into standardized, discrete, Minimalist-inspired units. To the tension between abstraction and representation, *Foundation* added an artificial/natural tension, and marked a shift toward an interest in the built environment that was continued in *Pier* (1994) and a host of unrealized pieces, such as *Dam, Causeway,* and *Spillway.*

The next series—*Foundation: East Kingston, Foundation: Malden, Foundation: Connelly,* and *Foundation: Esopus* (all 1993)—came out of a desire to connect the foundations to place and to get closer to my actual experience of finding foundations in the woods near my home. Each piece is a 24 x 24 x 4" aluminum-covered box in which are set four bricks in the form of a square. The bricks for each piece are taken from a foundation in the place for which the piece is named. I knew one of the foundations before the series began and found

Foundation: Connelly

Foundation: Malden

▲ Foundation of Light-colored Stones (Rondout Creek, Rosendale, NY)

▼ Foundation of Light-colored Ston‹

▲ Foundation of Light-colored Stones

Foundation of Light-colored Stones

the rest by exploring areas where there were likely to be foundations, mostly along the Hudson River and Rondout Creek, near Kingston, NY. *Malden* and *Esopus* were from the former sites of, respectively, the Staples and Schleede brickyards; *East Kingston* was a house foundation; and *Connelly* was probably the foundation of a storeroom or other outbuilding for the cement kiln nearby.

The outdoor, impermanent foundation installations, around which this book is based, continued this movement into the landscape, which was reinforced by my discovery of Robert Smithson, Robert Morris, Walter de Maria, Dennis Oppenheim, Michael Heizer, Alice Aycock, and other artists who emerged from Minimalism in the late sixties and early seventies. The concerns of these artists— archeology, the natural sciences, aesthetic theories of landscape, ruins—form the background of the foundations, and in the foreground is the find-arrange-photograph technique of the contemporary landscape artist Andy Goldsworthy, which gave me a way to engage these concerns on a smaller, more intimate scale.

The technique was simple. I would go for a walk with my camera and notebook, find and arrange materials into the rectangular form of a foundation, and photograph the result. This left me with a limited but adequate number of choices. I could go to places I knew or I could explore. I could use materials I found there, either natural or artificial, or I could bring them with me in the form of mason's line. I could photograph them from various positions. After the order and planning of my studio work, I found it liberating to have a project that was so open and off-hand and easy, one that I could think about and do intermittently and with almost no preparation, but which could draw in my various interests and build to something larger and more coherent than any of the separate pieces.

Most of the foundations are slight and improbable, a simple rearranging of the site, a focusing by minimal means, hovering between something there and nothing there. The experience of the piece requires and reinforces Ehrenzweig's "diffuse, scattered kind of attention," it requires the kind of artistic attention that created it. You can't really look *at* the piece—there isn't much there—you need to look *over* and *through* and *from* and *to* the piece, you need to move around and be in the space it creates, looking back and forth and getting different views.

▲ Foundation of Mason's Line I (Island Dock, Kingston, NY)
▼

Foundation of Mason's Line 1

All buildings at Çatal Hüyük [a Neolithic townsite in present-day Turkey, first occupied about 6500 BC] were constructed of sun-dried rectangular mud-bricks, reeds and plaster. The bricks were formed in a wooden mould squared with an adze. Stone is not found in the alluvial plain in which the site was situated and for foundations up to six courses of mud-brick were used, well sunk below the level of the floor.

...

Because of the habit of building one structure on top of the other, using the old walls as foundations, a certain homogeneity of plan was created, but by subdividing rooms or joining others together, by using the site of one or more rooms for creating a courtyard or open space, the plans of individual building-levels vary considerably even if the general layout is to a great extent preserved. It will eventually be of great interest to trace the plans of the successive building-levels down to the orginal master-plan which the conservative builders of Çatal Hüyük continued to follow through numerous centuries.

James Mellaart, *Çatal Hüyük: A Neolithic Town in Anatolia*

In the remains of the Schleede brickyard in Esopus, the foundations of the buildings are made of Schleede bricks. I love this idea of the brickyard built of its own bricks, so absurdly matter-of-fact and logical in its own way, like a Borges story. This feeling is reinforced a little further up the river, at a ruined cement plant, where all the foundations are of cement.

In Gordon Matta-Clark's *Splitting: Four Corners* he cut a house in half from roof to foundation, then pared away one cinderblock from the foundation over half the length of the house, allowing that half to tilt away from the other. It is this fineness amidst the devastation and disorder that I like.

The creative thinker is capable of alternating between differentiated and undifferentiated modes of thinking, harnessing them together to give him service for solving very definite tasks.
Anton Ehrenzweig, *The Hidden Order of Art*

In "Towards the Development of an Air Terminal Site," Robert Smithson focuses on construction projects and their value to artists, both as models for future artworks and as artistic experiences in themselves. After discussing the "aesthetic value" of boring holes in the ground, he anticipates many of the earth art projects of later years, by himself and others, when he says "Pavements, holes, trenches, mounds, heaps, paths, ditches, roads, terraces, etc., all have an esthetic potential." Later in the essay he elaborates on this, saying "The process behind the making of a storage facility may be viewed in stages, thus constituting a whole "series" of works of art from the ground up. Land surveying and preliminary building, if isolated into discrete stages, may be viewed as an array of artworks that vanish as they develop."

PILES of the LAKE DWELLING of MÖRINGEN.

*(Bronze Age.)*

As usual, Smithson raises more questions than he answers and suggests more than he states, but his point here is not to build anything substantial but rather to open up a space in which to project possibilities. He begins with an attraction to building sites and processes, then says that they have "an esthetic value," closing the gap between art and everyday activities. But, typically, Smithson doesn't say that building activities *are* art, but rather that they "may be viewed as" art. This appreciation of their "esthetic potential" is a middle term, a stage in the process, with his real interest being in what implications this viewing can have for artists, what space can be opened up and what projects suggested. Toward the end of the essay, Smithson writes "By investigating the physical forms of such projects one may gain unexpected esthetic information. I am not concerned here with the original functions of such massive projects, but rather with what they suggest or evoke." The movement of the essay, then, is from attraction to building practices to viewing them as art to conceiving and producing new art under their influence; or as Smithson might have expressed it, the dialectic between art and building practices can be used to produce new art.

Foundation for a maze

Foundation for a well

Foundation of rocks in river, half-submerged. Maybe have low end start at low tide line, filling would document tide level. At high tide low end would be right at surface.

Foundation of brick rubble

Foundation of removed stones, brick

Foundation in sand or mud at low tide, photo each hour

Foundation burned into grass

Foundation of trampled grass, mud

In setting out the foundations, it should be noted that the base of the wall and the plinth (which are also considered part of the foundation) must be somewhat wider than the proposed wall—for the very same reason for which people who walk through the snow in the Tuscan Alps strap to their feet rackets strung with cord, since the enlarged footprint will prevent them from sinking so much.
Leon Battista Alberti, *On the Art of Building in Ten Books*

Foundation of Trampled Mud (Kingston, NY)

▼ Foundation of Trampled Mud

▲ Foundation of Trampled Mud

▼ Foundation of Trampled Mu

So much of what happens below ground is unknown, that to entrust it with the responsibility of bearing a structural and financial burden can never be done without risk. And so, especially in the foundations, where more than anywhere else in the building the thought and attention of a careful and circumspect builder are required, nothing must be overlooked. A mistake elsewhere will cause less damage, and be less difficult to rectify and more easily borne, but in the foundations a mistake is inexcusable.
Leone Battista Alberti, *On the Art of Building in Ten Books*

I like the aerial, plan view, the foundation laid out whole below me, but this is not the defining view, it is not the product or goal, just one of the views I enjoy.

After photographing the foundations I was surprised to find how much I like the details. The view of an isolated corner seemed contradictory to the expansive nature of the piece, but I found that the details have the energy that I want the entire piece to have. They project out, completing their lines in space and have the paradoxical feeling I want of openness and containment.

▲ Foundation of Trampled Mud

▼ Foundation of Trampled M

**foun.da.tion** (foun da shen), n. **1.** that on which something is founded. **2.** the basis or groundwork of anything: *the moral founda-tion of both society and religion.* **3.** the natural or prepared ground on which some structure rests: *The blast shook the foundation of every building.* **4.** the lowest division of a building, wall, or the like, usu-ally of masonry and partly or wholly below the surface of the ground. **5.** act of founding, setting up, establishing, etc.: *a policy in effect since the foundation.* **6.** state of being founded. **7.** a donation or legacy for the support of an institution; an endowment: *to solicit foundations from alumni.* **8.** an endowed institution: *a private foundation for study abroad.* **9.** a cosmetic, as a cream or liquid, used as a base for facial make-up. **10.** see **foundation garment. 11.** *Solitaire.* a card or given denomination on which other cards are to be added according to denomination or suit. [ME *foundacioun* < L *fundation-* (s. of *fundatio*), equiv. to *fundat(us)* (ptp. of *fundare*; see FOUND) + *ion-* -ION] — **foun.da tion.al**, adj. —**foun. da tion.al.ly**, adj. **foun.da tion.ary**, adj.
—**Syn. 3.** See **base. 3, 4.** footing. **5, 6.** establishment, settlement.
—**Ant. 3, 4.** superstructure.
*Random House Dictionary of the English Language,* Random House, New York, 1971.


The digging of the foundations and their infilling, the raising of the wall and the laying of the covering, should all be conducted at dif-ferent times of the year and under different climatic conditions. The best moment to dig foundations is at the time of the Dog Star or during autumn itself, when the ground is dry and there is no water to flow into the trenches to impede the work. It is not at all unsuitable to fill in the foundations at the beginning of spring, espe-cially if they are deep, as the earth will stand by and give them

ROBENHAUSEN

Piles of the latest Settlement – Split Oak stems as seen 20 June 1865.

Foundation of Black Plastic Tubes (Eddyville, NY)

# Building and Foundation

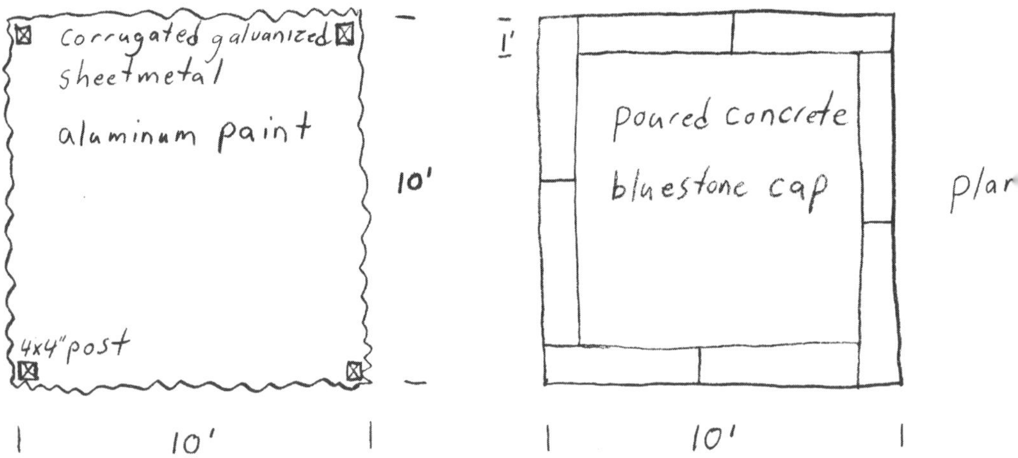

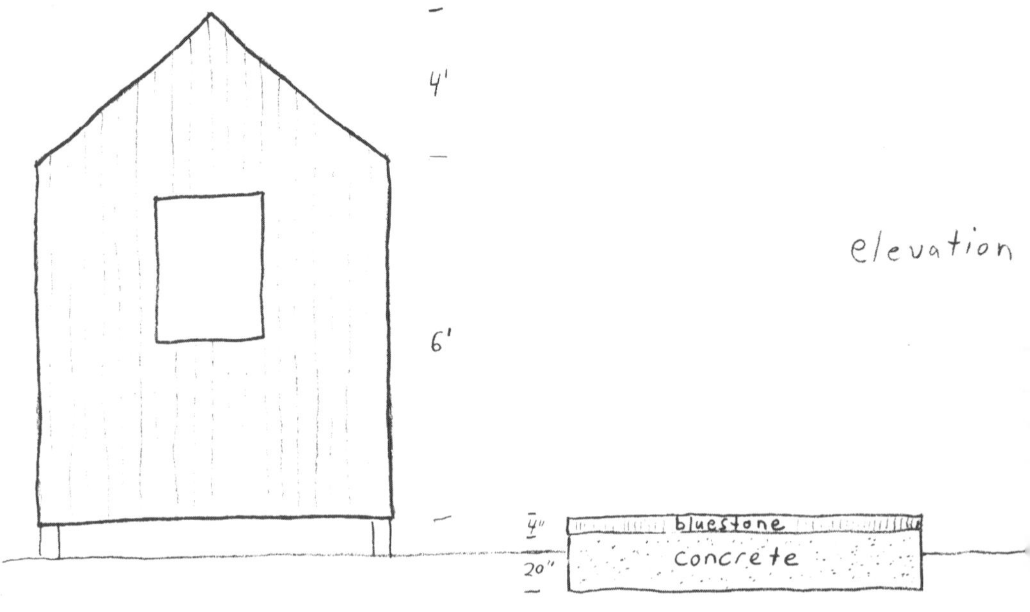

corrugated galvanized
sheetmetal

aluminum paint

4x4" post

10'

10'

I'

poured concrete
bluestone cap

plan

10'

4'

6'

elevation

bluestone

concrete

4"

20"

- gable roof
- 4x3' window each side
- set in grassy field, 10' or so between
  parts, depending on site

sufficient protection from the heat of the summer. The beginning of winter, however, is by far the best time to fill them in, except in polar regions and other cold places, where they will immediately freeze rather than set.

Leon Battista Alberti, *On the Art of Building in Ten Books*


For fortified towns the following general principles are to be observed. First comes the choice of a very healthy site. Such a site will be high, neither misty nor frosty, and in a climate neither hot nor cold, but temperate; further, without marshes in the neighborhood. For when the morning breezes blow toward the town at sunrise, if they bring with them mists from marshes and, mingled with the mist, the poisonous breath of creatures of the marshes to be wafted into the bodies of the inhabitants, they will make the site unhealthy. Again, if the town is on the coast with a southern or western exposure, it will not be healthy, because in summer the southern sky grows hot at sunrise and is fiery at noon, while a western exposure grows warm after sunrise, is hot at noon, and at evening all aglow.

Vitruvius, *The Ten Books of Architecture*

Smithson's non-site is a way to contain the "oceanic" nature of the site, to set limits. It is a three-dimensional map, a container, itself a fragment, that contains fragments of the site. It both presents and represents the site.

I have been trying to define the experience of being in the piece, moving through its space, but this is an experience that only I have had. How does my experience relate to the experience of the photographs? Smithson speaks of the non-sites as "the residue of an activity." What is left in the photographs of my activity? How do the photographs function and what part do my verbal descriptions play? Are they part of the piece? I haven't thought so, or at least not in an individual sense of photographs and text comprising a particular foundation. But the text I am working on does have a relation, as yet unspecified, to the foundations, one that is not simply on an explanatory, subsidiary level. Taking Ehrenzweig's cue, I need to allow myself to write as I work, and expect this type of attention from the reader. This is my only choice. My interests are diffuse and can be drawn out and elaborated, but not at the expense of their sometimes fragile, tenuous connections.

*Dimini*   *Plan showing the general topography of the neolithic acropolis .*

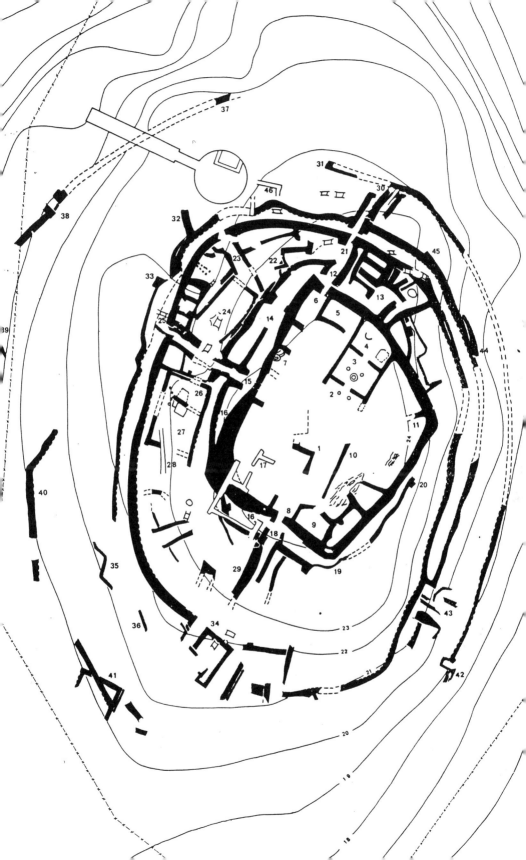

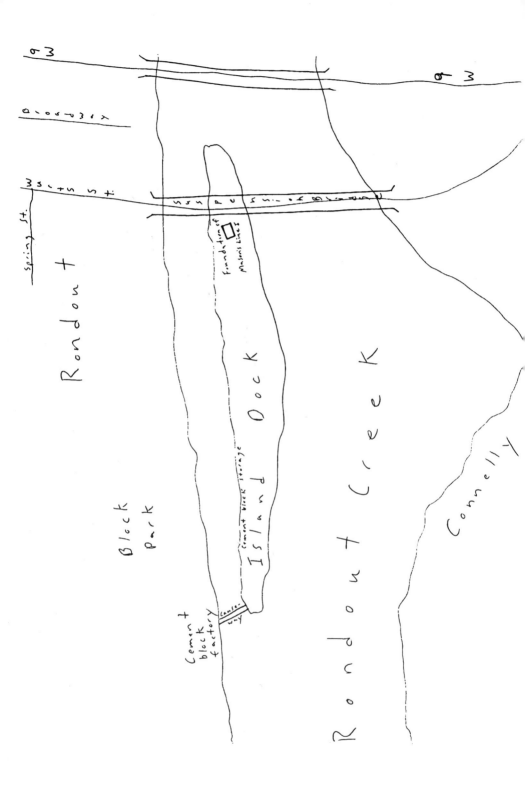

*Map 1   Foundation of Mason's Line I*

Foundation of Mason's Line I

There remains but a single wall-painting to be described, which more than any other illustrates the artistic genius of the people of Çatal Hüyük. Painted on the north and east wall of a shrine (VII. 14) of Level VII, soon after 6200 BC according to radiocarbon dating, it represents that rarest genre of early painting, a landscape, and needless to say it is unique. In the foreground is shown a town with rectangular houses clearly indicated. Each house has its own walls and they are placed one next to the other without any open spaces. The rows of houses rise in terraces up to the top of the mound (as in the section of Level VI B and no doubt VII also).

Beyond the town and much smaller as if far away, rises a double peaked mountain covered with dots and from its base parallel lines extend. More lines erupt from its higher peak and more dots are grouped beyond its right slope and in horizontal rows above its peak, interspersed with horizontal and vertical lines. A clearer picture of a volcano in eruption could hardly have been painted: the fire coming out of the top, lava streams from vents at its base, clouds of smoke and glowing ash hanging over its peak and raining down on and beyond the slopes of the volcano are all combined in the painting. It is not difficult to localize this picture: Hasan Dağ (10,673 feet) is the only twin peaked volcano in Central Anatolia and it lies at the eastern end of the Konya Plain, within view of Çatal Hüyük. James Mellaart, *Çatal Hüyük*

This is apparently the earliest known landscape painting and the earliest known city plan. That is, it is the earliest realistic evocation of a place along with the earliest abstract representation of the dwellings there. As such, this painting could function as an emblem of all my work with foundations, a point of focus for the tensions and reverberations that are set up by placing human-built structures in the landscape.

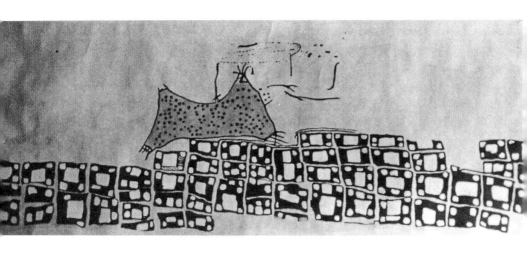

59, 60 Copy and original of a landscape painting from north and east walls of shrine VII.14. In the foreground is a town rising in graded terraces closely packed with rectangular houses. Behind the town an erupting volcano is shown, its sides covered with incandescent volcanic bombs rolling down the slope of the mountain. Others are thrown up from the erupting cone above which hovers a cloud of smoke and ashes. The twin cones suggest that an eruption of Hasan Dağ, rising to a height of 10,672 feet (3,553 metres) and standing at the eastern end of the Konya Plain and visible from Çatal Hüyük, is recorded. *See* Plate I

▲ Foundation of Bricks on Mudflat (Kingston, NY)

FOUNDATION. ...Laying the foundation of a city or a temple was an elaborate ceremony in the ancient Middle East. At times it was accompanied by human sacrifice (Josh. 6:26; I Kings 16:34). Inscribed cylinders were placed in some Babylonian foundations. In excavations frequently remains of foundations show ground plans where the superstructure has been destroyed.

*The Interpreter's Dictionary of the Bible*

Foundation document of Adad-nirari I (1305-1274 B.C.)

This stone tablet is just one example of the magnificent inscriptions Adad-nirari I commissioned for his building projects....

Because of the countless foundation documents he commissioned, evidenced by the large number that survive, this ruler has a unique place in literary history. His building and restoration efforts are documented on 58 stone slabs, 12 clay tablets, and no fewer than 170 bricks—to name only the most common types of inscription of this kind. There are also clay cones, cylinders, cornerstones; alabaster vessels and other objects in stone; and an axe and a bronze sword that is now in the Metropolitan Museum.

The king's favorite project was the temple of the goddess Ishtar Ashuritu, the Assyrian Ishtar, worshipped at Ashur since Early Dynastic times. Built of sun-dried bricks, such structures deteriorated rapidly and required constant upkeep. Accordingly, one of a ruler's most noble tasks was to provide for the preservation of important shrines. In so doing he brought honor to himself as well as to the god in question. In royal epithets the term "restorer" became a literary topos.

In the course of such undertakings kings paid particular attention to the similar efforts of their predecessors. By the time of Adad-nirari I, the tradition of giving public structures appropriate foundation documents was already thousands of years old. Royal workmen carefully searched for documents from the past and treated the ones they found according to admonitions included in the texts. Among the reasons for this was their fear of the curses contained in the texts, which called for the direst punishments of those who mistreated such documents.

Accordingly, after listing his titles and epithets on the present tablet, Adad-nirari I recounted the structure's long history: "At that time the temple of the Assyrian Ishtar, my mistress, which Ilu-shumma, vice-regent of Ashur, my forefather, son of Shalim-ahum [who was] also vice-regent of Ashur, had previously built and completed— that temple became dilapidated and Sargon [I], vice-regent of Ashur, son of Ikunum [who was] also vice-regent of Ashur, restored it; again it became dilapidated and Puzur-Ashur [III], vice-regent of Ashur, my forefather, son of Ashur-nirari [I, who was] also vice-regent of Ashur, restored it—that temple, its towers, the room of the *shuhuru* of the courtyard, the storeroom of the goddess Ishtar of

# Foundation of Cement

```
c e m e n t c e m e n t c e m e n t c e m e n t
e m e n t c e m e n t c e m e n t c e m e n t c
m e n t c e m e n t c e m e n t c e m e n t c e
e n t c e m e n t c e m e n t c e m e n t c e m
n t c e m e n t c e m e n t c e m e n t c e m e
t c e m e n t c e m e n t c e m e n t c e m e n
c e m e n t                         c e m e n t
e m e n t c                         e m e n t c
m e n t c e                         m e n t c e
e n t c e m                         e n t c e m
n t c e m e                         n t c e m e
t c e m e n                         t c e m e n
c e m e n t                         c e m e n t
e m e n t c                         e m e n t c
m e n t c e                         m e n t c e
e n t c e m                         e n t c e m
n t c e m e                         n t c e m e
t c e m e n                         t c e m e n
c e m e n t                         c e m e n t
e m e n t c                         e m e n t c
m e n t c e                         m e n t c e
e n t c e m                         e n t c e m
n t c e m e                         n t c e m e
t c e m e n                         t c e m e n
c e m e n t                         c e m e n t
e m e n t c                         e m e n t c
m e n t c e                         m e n t c e
e n t c e m                         e n t c e m
n t c e m e                         n t c e m e
t c e m e n                         t c e m e n
c e m e n t c e m e n t c e m e n t c e m e n t
e m e n t c e m e n t c e m e n t c e m e n t c
m e n t c e m e n t c e m e n t c e m e n t c e
e n t c e m e n t c e m e n t c e m e n t c e m
n t c e m e n t c e m e n t c e m e n t c e m e
t c e m e n t c e m e n t c e m e n t c e m e n
```

plan

```
c e m e n t            c e m e n t
```

lat. cross-section

```
c e m e n t                         c e m e n t
```

long cross-section

the courtyard which is called the 'Inn of the Goddess Ishtar,' and the room of the goddess Ishara of the courtyard had again become dilapidated...."

He then detailed his own restoration, expressly noting his strengthening of the foundations....

Prudence Oliver Harper, *Assyrian Origins: Discoveries at Ashur on the Tigris*

...ruins in reverse, that is—all the new construction that would eventually be built. This is the opposite of the "romantic ruin" because the buildings don't fall into ruin after they are built but rather rise into ruin before they are built.

Robert Smithson, "A Tour of the Monument of Passaic, New Jersey"


In these terms, my proposals for more permanent projects suggest either the beginning or the end of this building process, either the foundation for a forthcoming building or the foundation of a building that has disappeared, leaving only the artwork, its trace and footprint.

Even in the proposals for permanent pieces, I'm not interested in excavating the interior space, it is unnecessary. In terms of time and Smithson's musings, it is as if the interior space has filled in over time or has yet to be excavated, which is much the same thing. There is a concern with time, but not with the usual perception of it as flowing forward. This forward movement is neutralized. The work is disorienting (a spatial metaphor—what is the time term?), it goes forward and backward in time, anticipating a building and evidencing a past building. It is an opening up of possibility and an end to possibility.

The result of this disorientation, this blurring of past and future, is that the work exists in an expanded present that encompasses both past and future. This is always true of the present, but this type of work gives the present even more elasticity, it calls attention to the constructed nature of our relation to time and reconstructs it.

This type of work is also disorienting in terms of space because it has definite, contained, condensed interior space, but an uncontained, unlimited exterior space, one that has no boundaries other than those of the site. The site of the work, the physical space it takes up and takes in, is determined by the range of sight of the viewer, and is constantly changing as the viewer moves. The viewer is thus always in the work and determines it by his or her presence in and perception of it.

This has ramifications for the photography of these works.

Foundation of Sumac II (The Commons, Kingston, NY)

▲ Foundation of Apple Branches (Ulster Park, NY)
▼

Foundation of Mason's Line I (Island Dock, Kingston, NY)

▲ Foundation of Light-colored Stones (Rosendale, NY)

▼ Foundation of Cattails (Eddyville, N

Foundation of Yellow Leaves (Marbletown, NY)

▼ Foundation of Mason's Line II (Kingston, NY)

Foundation of Sumac II

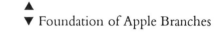 Foundation of Apple Branches

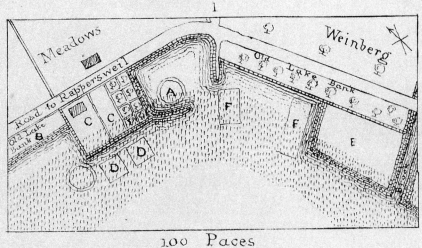

1

Meadows

Weinberg

Old Lake Bank

Road to Rapperswei

Old Lake Bank

A

B

C  C

F

F

D  D

D  D

E

100 Paces

GROUND PLAN

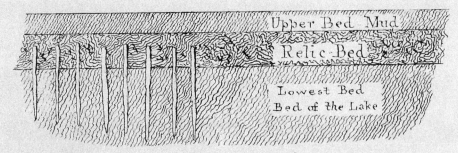

2

Water

Upper Bed Mud

Relic Bed

Lowest Bed
Bed of the Lake

SECTION

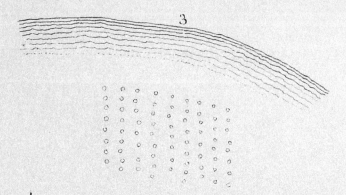

3

ARRANGEMENT OF THE PILES

# Boathouse Foundation I

Plan

- wood piles, 1' across, set 4' apart on center, 20' square overall
- set in shallow water, a little away from shore, top of piles 1' above surface of water

The design of the foundations must vary therefore according to the site. Some sites may be high up, others down low, and others in between these, such as slopes, for example; then again, some may be parched and arid, especially mountain ridges and summits, and others utterly saturated and damp, such as those which lie on the coast, by a lagoon, or in a valley. Others may remain neither totally dry nor utterly wet, because they are positioned on a slope, which is true for any place where water does not remain still and stagnant but always runs downhill.

Leone Battista Alberti, *On the Art of Building in Ten Books*

Had idea while going to sleep last night of removing all the sculpture at Storm King, having a show of the traces that remain, the foundations of the pieces, the concrete slabs and iron bolts and holes in the ground.

Foundation in marsh

Foundation of rubber mats

Foundation of fire—burning wood or candles or solid fuel tablets. Could also be done on water, floating candles, or foundation going from water to land.

# FOUNDATION

Is *the ground-work, or lowest part of a building, which supports the other parts; as the foundation of an house, of a castle, of a fort, tower, &c.* Christ Jesus, *both in the Old and New Testament, is called a* Foundation. *Isa.* 28. 16, Behold, I lay in Zion for a foundation, a stone, a tried stone, a precious corner-stone, a sure foundation.

*And in Rom.* 15. 20, *The apostle says,* So I have strived to preach the gospel, not where Christ was named, lest I should build upon another man's foundation.

*Exod.* 9. 18. as hath been in Egypt since the *f.*
*Josh.* 6. 26. he shall lay the *f.* in his firstborn
1 *Kings* 5. 17. they brought hewn stones to lay the *f.*
  6. 87. in the fourth year was *f.* of L. laid
  7. 9. were of costly stones even from the *f.*
2 *Chron.* 31. 7. they began to lay the *f.* of the heaps
*Ezra* 3. 6. the *f.* of the temple was not yet laid
*Job* 4. 19. how much less in them whose *f.* is in dust
  22. 16. whose *f.* was overflown with a flood
*Psal.* 87. 1. his *f.* is in the holy mountains
  102. 25. of old thou hast laid the *f.* of the earth
  137. 7. rase it, rase it, even to the *f.* thereof
*Ezek.* 13. 14. the *f.* thereof shall be discovered
*Hag.* 2. 18. from the day that the *f.* was laid
*Zech.* 12. 1. the Lord, which layeth the *f.* of the earth
*Luke* 6. 48. digged deep, and laid the *f.* on a rock
  49. like a man that without a *f.* built a house
1 *Cor.* 3. 10. as a wise master-builder I laid the *f.*
  11. for other *f.* can no man lay than is laid
  12. if any man build on this *f.* gold, silver, wood

*A Complete Concordance to the Holy Scriptures of the Old and New Testaments,* Alexander Cruden, compiler

Foundation on train tracks—stone or brick or grass

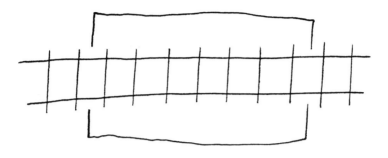

photo from overpass or signal tower

Boathouse Foundation

Foundation of bridge, concrete or stone piers

Foundation of white calcium-covered stones in cave

Foundation of fire in lake in cave

Foundation of roofing slates, end to end or a few deep

Foundation of bricks in river

Thought while walking along the shore of the river, past the sites of brickyards that have long since disappeared, that the bricks littering the beach are like a dispersed, linear foundation.

The changing brick brands—from Rose to Hutton to Washburn to Terry to Brophy to Staples—are like an interconnected foundation that points back in time to the brickyards that used to line the shore and the families that owned them.

Buried foundation—make foundation, bury, photograph

Foundation of shells

Cut or find piles, set up foundation in marsh near Kingston Point Park

crannog

Pfahlbauten

habitations lacustres

pile dwellings

When I was growing up there were a number of old boathouses, in various states of repair, along the shore of Mohegan Lake. Some were still used, others crumbling into the water and home to swallows, still others marked only by a few piles poking out of the water or strewn in the shallows.

▲ Foundation of Yellow Leaves (Marbletown, NY)

▼ Foundation of Yellow Lea

207 Hurley

Esopus

arbletown

Rt40 209

M

a

r

S

h

Foundation of
red leaves

Foundation of
yellow leaves

rail trail
(former railroad bed)

Rosendale

Lucas Turnpike

York

Binnewater

First

Second

Third

Fourth

*p 2   Foundations of Red Leaves and Yellow Leaves*

Foundation of Red Leaves (Marbletown, NY)

Foundation of Red Leaves

# GENERAL FORM.

Before proceeding to a description of the different lake dwellings, and of the objects found in them, it may be well in the first place to give an idea of the general form of these singular settlements, and of the different varieties under which they may be classed. The substructure will naturally claim our first attention.

## I. SUBSTRUCTURE.

I. Pile Dwellings.—What may especially be called the pile dwellings are by far the most numerous in the lakes of Switzerland and Upper Italy. The annexed woodcut will give

Fig. 1.

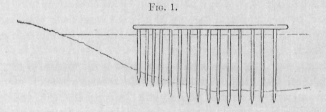

a general notion of the arrangement: piles of various kinds of wood, sometimes split, but in general mere stems with the bark on, sharpened sometimes by fire, sometimes by stone hatchets or celts, and in later times by tools of bronze and probably of iron, were driven into the shallows of the lakes, provided they were not rocky, at various distances from the shore. These piles were placed sometimes close together, sometimes in pairs, sometimes tolerably wide apart—generally in regular order, but occasionally in apparent confusion. In all cases the heads of the piles were brought to a level, and then the platform beams were laid upon them, which in some cases were fastened by wooden pins, in others mortises or central hollows were cut in the heads of the vertical piles to receive the cross beams. Occasionally cross timbers were joined to the upright piles below the platform to support and steady the structure, either forced in, as it were, between them, or fastened to them by what workmen call 'notching,' that is, portions were cut out of the vertical piles to receive the cross timbers. The platform lying on the top of this series of piles appears in many cases to have been of the rudest construction, and to have consisted merely of one or two layers of unbarked stems lying parallel one to another; in a few cases, as in one of the Italian lake dwellings, they were more artificial, and were composed of boards, split out of the trunks of trees, and joined with some approach to accuracy.

In many cases the outer row of piles appears to have been covered or closed in by a kind of wattle or hurdle work, made of small twigs or branches, probably to lessen the splash of the water, or to prevent the piles from being injured by floating wood.

The distance from the shore as before mentioned varied considerably : there appears to have been no regular rule in this respect ; it may, however, be well to mention that when a lake dwelling has been inhabited both in the stone and the bronze age, that part evidently used in the bronze age is frequently further from shore and deeper in the lake than that which belongs to the age of stone. With this exception, as far as can be ascertained, nearly the same mode of construction prevailed in the pile dwellings during the ages of stone, bronze, and iron.

Some few of these dwellings appear to have almost touched the shore, but this is not a common case : most of them, as before mentioned, are at some little distance from it, and in all probability they were connected with it by a narrow platform or bridge formed also on piles ; in some lake dwellings the remains of these bridge-like entrances have actually been discovered.

In certain cases, as near Nidau, &c., these pile dwellings have another peculiarity : they are formed on artificial elevations at the bottom of the lake, made by a large number of stones, which have evidently been brought in boats, and sunk on the spot for some especial purpose ; in fact, one boat or canoe, still loaded with the stones which proved too great a cargo for it, and which consequently sunk it to the bottom, is still to be seen at Peters Island in the lake of Bienne ; the particulars will be given when this locality is described. These artificial mounds or hillocks, under the surface of the water, are not uncommon, especially in the western lakes, and all go by the name of Stein-berg. The woodcut (fig. 2) gives some idea of this variety of pile dwelling.

▲ Foundation of Red Leaves
▼

Foundation of Yellow Leaves

Foundation of Yellow Leaves

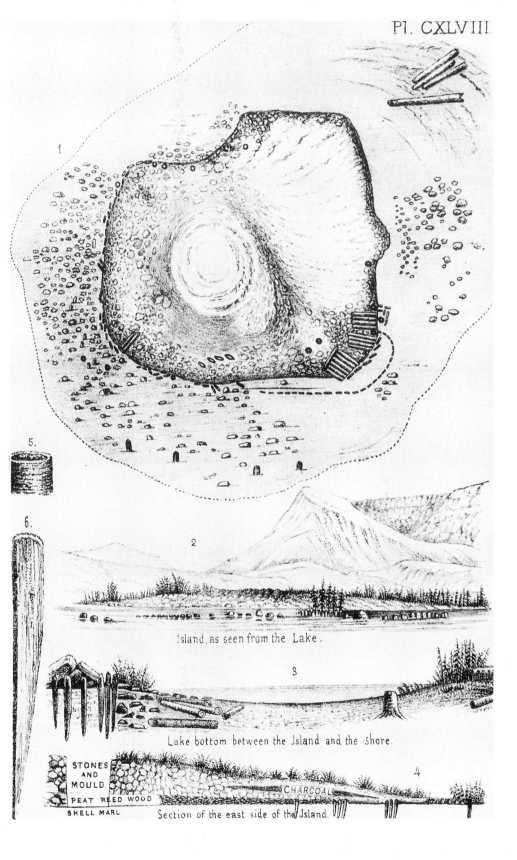

Pl. CXLVIII.

Island, as seen from the Lake.

Lake bottom between the Island and the Shore.

STONES AND MOULD

PEAT REED WOOD

SHELL MARL

CHARCOAL

Section of the east side of the Island.

As it seems impossible, according to the opinions of the best engineers, to drive piles into a regular heap of stones, we are obliged to come to the conclusion that the piles must first have been driven more or less deeply into the mud, and that the stones were afterwards thrown down between and around the piles, in order to consolidate the erection.[1]

FIG. 2.

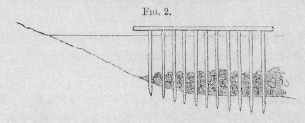

II. FRAME PILE DWELLINGS.—The expression frame dwellings, though not very elegant, perhaps explains the peculiar structure better than any other. This form is comparatively rare, and though it has been said to occur in other places, yet we can only actually refer to two or three settlements in the lake of Zürich. The distinction between this form and the regular pile settlement consists in the fact that the piles, instead of having been driven into the mud of the lake, had been fixed by a mor-

FIG. 3.

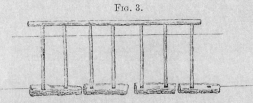

tise and tenon arrangement into split trunks, lying horizontally on the bottom of the lake. This plan was chiefly followed where the bottom of the lake consisted of very soft mud, such as would hardly allow of a hold for the piles. In such a case the flat split trunks would be very useful. The above diagram shows the mode in which the plan was applied,

[1] An engineering friend informs me that an arrangement of a similar kind has been used on a much larger scale in the new pier at Portland. Here long piles are driven and screwed down into the tenacious clay, forming the bottom, till they are sufficiently strong to bear a kind of railroad. Huge masses of rock are then brought upon it in trams from Portland Isle, and thrown down between and around the piles, so as to form a regular breakwater against the heavy seas which beat on that coast. I am also informed by the engineer of the harbour of refuge at Holyhead, that precisely the same plan is adopted there with their long piles, except that they are not screwed but driven in to support the stage from which the stone is thrown.—[TR.]

and the annexed woodcut is a sketch of one of the actual beams brought up from the bottom. Several of these stems,

FIG. 4.

with holes in them, are known to be lying on the bottom of many of the Swiss lakes, so that it is *possible* that this form of structure may have been more common than we at present imagine.

III. FASCINE DWELLINGS.—Some lake dwellings were of very peculiar structure, and may be designated fascine dwellings. Instead of a platform, supported on a series of piles, these erections consisted of layers of sticks, or small stems of trees built up from the bottom of the lake, till the structure reached above the water mark; and on this series of layers the main platform for the huts was placed. Numerous upright piles are indeed found in dwellings of this description, but they were not used to support the platform as in the pile dwellings just mentioned, but chiefly as stays or guides for the great mass of sticks, in successive layers, which reached down to the bottom of the lake. The woodcut annexed shows a section of a lake

FIG. 5.

dwelling built on this peculiar plan. As several settlements of this kind will be carefully described in the course of the following pages, it will be unnecessary at present to enter into further detail. It may, however, be well to mention that fascine dwellings occur chiefly in the smaller lakes, and apparently belong to the stone age.

from *Lake Dwellings,* Ferdinand Keller

# Boathouse Foundation II

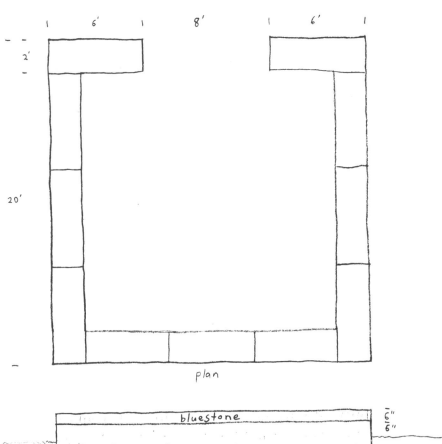

plan

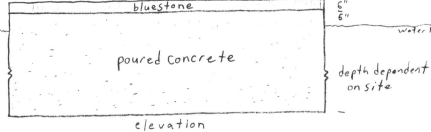

elevation

— set in river, lake, or artificial pond

Foundation of Cattails (Eddyville, NY)

Foundation of Cattails ▶

Foundation of Cattails

▼ Foundation of Cattails

If, however, solid ground cannot be found, but the place proves to be nothing but a heap of loose earth to the very bottom, or a marsh, then it must be dug up and cleared out and set with piles made of charred alder or olive wood or oak, and these piles must be driven down by machinery, very closely together like a bridge—piles, and the intervals between them filled in with charcoal, and finally the foundations are to be laid on them in the most solid form of construction. The foundations having been brought up to the level, the stylobates are next to be put in place.

Vitruvius, *The Ten Books of Architecture*

## Section at the Lake Dwelling of Robenhausen, October 1864.

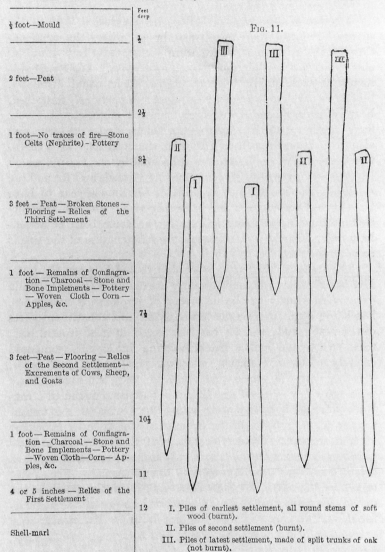

Fig. 11.

| | |
|---|---|
| ½ foot—Mould | Feet deep |
| | ½ |
| 2 feet—Peat | |
| | 2½ |
| 1 foot—No traces of fire—Stone Celts (Nephrite) – Pottery | |
| | 3½ |
| 3 feet — Peat — Broken Stones — Flooring — Relics of the Third Settlement | |
| 1 foot — Remains of Conflagration — Charcoal — Stone and Bone Implements — Pottery — Woven Cloth — Corn — Apples, &c. | |
| | 7¼ |
| 3 feet—Peat — Flooring — Relics of the Second Settlement— Excrements of Cows, Sheep, and Goats | |
| | 10½ |
| 1 foot — Remains of Conflagration — Charcoal — Stone and Bone Implements — Pottery —Woven Cloth—Corn— Apples, &c. | |
| | 11 |
| 4 or 5 inches — Relics of the First Settlement | |
| | 12 |
| Shell-marl | |

I. Piles of earliest settlement, all round stems of soft wood (burnt).

II. Piles of second settlement (burnt).

III. Piles of latest settlement, made of split trunks of oak (not burnt).

I grew up in Mohegan Lake, New York, and from the age of six or seven would go exploring with neighborhood kids in the area of woods we called Loyola, named for the seminary set at the far edge of the woods. Though it was completely covered in trees, the area had been cleared at one time and was scattered with traces of its former occupation—stone walls, strands of barbed wire embedded in old trees, the remains of houses and root cellars, a dump full of patent medicine bottles and milk pails and cow bones. Inside the ruin of what had probably been a barn, its exterior brick walls all that marked the space of what had been a large building, there was a rectangular pool of dark water about six by three feet, edged in brick, that we called The Bottomless Pool. There was a dead body in it, presumably still sinking into its bottomlessness. Years later I went back there and stuck a tree branch in it, pushing it down into the water as far as I could without hitting anything. I got a longer branch and was able to touch bottom. It was about three feet deep.

The logic of sculpture, it would seem is inseparable from the logic of monument. By virtue of this logic a sculpture is a commemorative representation. It sits in a particular place and speaks in a symbolical tongue about the meaning or use of that place.

…

With these two sculptural projects [Rodin's *Gates of Hell* and *Balzac*], I would say, one crosses the threshold of the logic of the monument, entering the space of what could be called its negative condition—a kind of sitelessness, or homelessness, an absolute loss of place. Which is to say one enters modernism, since it is the modernist period of sculptural production that operates in relation to this loss of site, producing the monument as abstraction, the monument as pure marker or base, functionally placeless and largely self-referential.

It is these two characteristics of modernist sculpture that declare its status and therefore its meaning and function, as essentially nomadic. Through its fetishization of the base, the sculpture reaches downward to absorb the pedestal into itself and away from actual place; and through the representation of its own materials or the process of its construction, the sculpture depicts its own autonomy.

Rosalind Kraus, "Sculpture in the Expanded Field"

Krauss defines modernist sculpture as being what is in front of the building but not the building and in the landscape but not the landscape. From these terms "architecture" and "landscape," and their conjunctions and contradictions, she generates what she calls the expanded field of postmodern sculpture, which very neatly maps the space in which my foundation project operates.

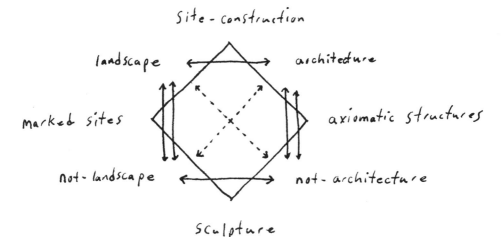

For a while when I was twelve or thirteen I wanted to be an archeologist, the only thing I ever wanted to be besides a writer. This was provoked by doing some digging in a stone foundation in Fahnstock State Park in Putnam County, New York, where my family would go hiking. There had been iron mines there in the nineteenth century, and Thomas Edison had lived just up the road from this foundation when he was trying to find the right alloy for the filament for his electric lightbulb. We only went digging twice, I think, but it had a strong effect on me. I dug in a corner of the foundation and found, besides the usual assortment of nails, an iron belt buckle with traces of silver and an 1865 penny.

ouse Foundation, Sodom Road, Marlboro, VT. Photo © 1997 Forrest Holzapfel.

Of the passion caused by the SUBLIME

The passion caused by the great and sublime in nature, when those causes operate most powerfully, is Astonishment; and astonishment is the state of the soul, in which all its motions are suspended, with some degree of horror. In this case the mind is so entirely filled with its object, that it cannot entertain any other, nor by consequence reason on that object which employs it. Hence arises the great power of the sublime, that far from being produced by them, it anticipates our reasonings, and hurries us on by an irresistible force.

TERROR

POWER

PRIVATION

VASTNESS

INFINITY

Infinity has a tendency to fill the mind with that sort of delightful horror which is the most genuine effect, and truest test of the sublime. There are scarce any things which can become the objects of our senses that are really, and in their own nature infinite. But the eye not being able to perceive the bounds of many things, they seem to be infinite, and they produce the same effects as if they were really so. We are deceived in the like manner, if the parts of some large object are so continued to any indefinite number, that the imagination meets no check which may hinder its extending them at pleasure.

## SUCCESSION and UNIFORMITY

Succession and uniformity of parts, are what constitute the artificial infinite. 1. *Succession;* which is requisite that the parts may be continued so long and in such a direction, as by their frequent impulses on the sense to impress the imagination with the idea of their progress beyond their actual limits. 2. *Uniformity;* because if the figures of the parts should be changed, the imagination at every change finds a check; you are presented at every alteration with the termination of one idea, and the beginning of another; by which means it becomes impossible to continue that uninterrupted progression, which alone can stamp on bounded objects the character of infinity.

...

To avoid the perplexity of general notions; let us set before our eyes a collonade of uniform pillars planted in a right line; let us take our stand, in such a manner, that the eye may shoot along this collonade, for it has its best effect in this view. In our present situation it is plain, that the rays from the first round pillar will cause in the eye a vibration of that species; an image of the pillar itself. The pillar immediately succeeding increases it; that which follows renews and enforces the impression; each in its order as it succeeds, repeats impulse after impulse, and stroke after stroke, until the eye long exercised in one particular way cannot lose that object immediately; and being violently roused by this continued agitation, it presents the mind with a grand or sublime conception.

Edmund Burke, *A Philosophical Inquiry into the Origin of our Ideas of the Sublime and Beautiful*

More concisely, the Beautiful is nature or art obeying the laws of perfect existence (i.e. Beauty) easily, freely, harmoniously, and without the *display* of power. The Picturesque is nature or art obeying the same laws rudely, violently, irregularly, and often displaying power only. Hence we find all Beautiful forms characterized by curved and flowing lines—lines expressive of infinity, of grace and willing obedience: and all Picturesque forms characterized by irregular and broken lines—lines expressive of violence, abrupt action, and partial disobedience, a struggling of the idea with the substance or the condition of its being.

Alexander Jackson Downing, *Landscape Gardening* (1841)

The foundations seem to operate in the space between the sublime and the beautiful, and thus to be aligned with the picturesque and Smithson's "dialectical landscape."

Inherent in the theories of Price and Gilpin, and in Olmsted's response to them, are the beginnings of a dialectic of the landscape. Burke's notion of "beautiful" and "sublime" functions as a thesis of smoothness, gentle curves, and delicacy of nature, and as an antithesis of terror, solitude, and vastness of nature, both of which are rooted in the real world, rather than in a Hegelian Ideal. Price and Gilpin provide a synthesis with their formulation of the "picturesque," which is on closer examination related to chance and change in the material order of nature. The contradictions of the "picturesque" depart from a static formalistic view of nature. The picturesque, far from being an inner movement of the mind, is based on real land; it precedes the mind in its material external existence. We cannot take a one-sided view of the landscape within this dialectic. A park can no longer be seen as "a thing-in-itself," but rather as a process of ongoing relationships existing in a physical region—the park becomes a "thing-for-us."…Dialectics of this type are a way of seeing things in a manifold of relations, not as isolated objects.

Robert Smithson, "Frederick Law Olmsted and the Dialectical Landscape"


Like the picturesque of painter, landscape architect, and builder of architectural ruins Hubert Robert (1733-1808), the foundations are suggestive of the transience of human constructions in nature. There is a feeling of the foundations' tenuous presence on the land and their imminent erasure by natural forces of wind and water.

Hubert Robert: *Le Temple de la Philosophie* in Le Jardin D'Ermenonville ▶

But though the foundations suggest the picturesque and evoke some of its elegiac, melancholic tone, they quickly disperse this feeling by their extreme transience. Robert's work is about the *idea* of the transience of human marks on nature. It suggests and evokes an atmosphere of transience but does not embody it, being constructed of the lasting materials of oil paint and stone. His paintings are as permanent as any others, and the ruins are as solidly constructed as any building. The foundations, in contrast, both evoke human transience and embody it, lasting only a few minutes or hours or days.

Irony seems key here. Robert provokes the viewer to meditate on transience by providing a simulation of transience in durable form. In a similarly ironic way, I want to suggest the feelings associated with the picturesque—change, loss, the interplay of human and natural forces—but then disperse those feelings by the work's extreme fragility, short duration, and ease of construction. Against Robert's ruined castles and aqueducts, which suggest laborious construction, grand habitation, and long decay, I place a foundation of flowerheads, which was assembled, photographed, and dispersed by the wind in the space of half an hour.

Foundation of Flowerheads (The Commons, Kingston, NY) ▶

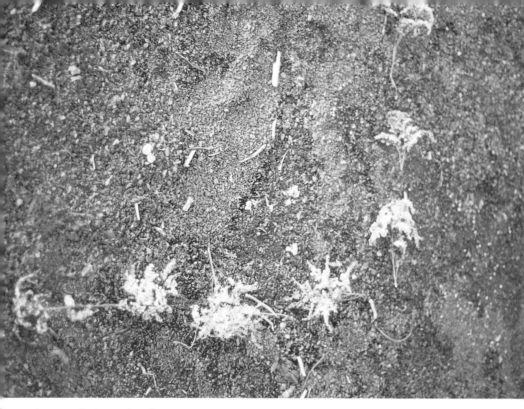

Foundation of Flowerheads

▼ Foundation of Flowerheads

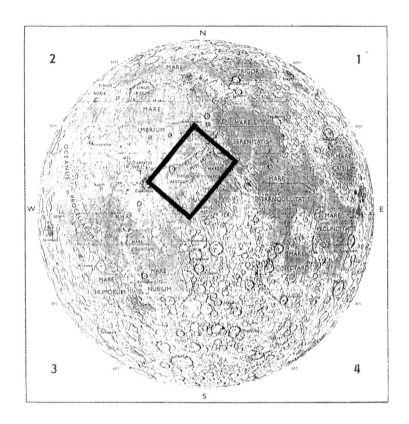

Spurred by the example of James Turrell's Roden *Crater Project*, I want to propose *Foundation on the Surface of the Moon*. It will be visible from earth and will be formed by blasting a trench into the surface of the moon, as follows: beginning the first corner at the Archimedes crater, proceed SW to Copernicus crater; then SE to the large crater W of the Sinus Medii; then NE to a crater at the intersection of Mare Serenitatis, Mare Tranquillitatis, and Mare Vaporum; then NW back to the Archimedes crater.

The wisdom of such an arrangement is plain. The incorporation of the Mare Vaporum is particularly apt, as is its siting sufficiently far from the Mare Humorum.

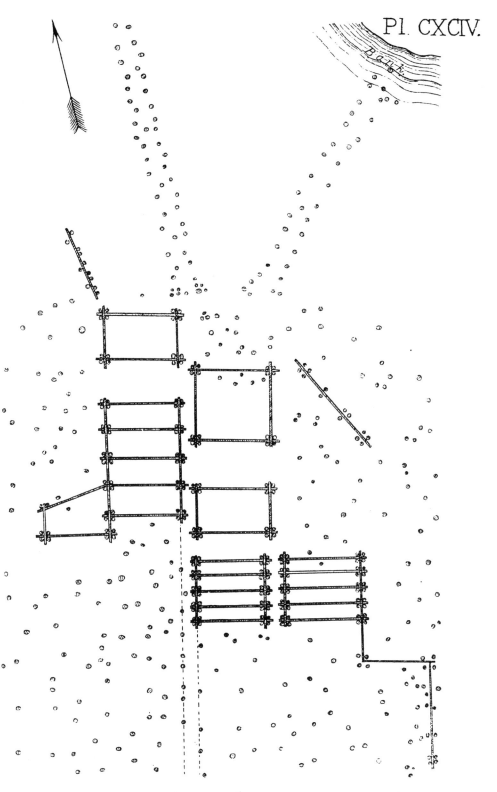

Pl. CXCIV.

GRANDS ROSEAUX.(Lake of Paladru.)

SCALE.— $\frac{1}{300}$.

An idea, as new as it was daring came to me. I would create build-
ings that gave the illusion of being buried.... As I considered the
problem, I realized that only low and sunken lines would be appro-
priate. After pondering on the rule that the first element of archi-
tecture is a wall totally bare and unadorned, I decided that my sunken
architecture would be exemplified in a building that was satisfactory
as a whole yet gave the appearance that part of it was below ground.
Etienne-Louis Boullee (1728-99) on his "sunken architecture"

In his "Funerary Monument" he does this by designing a building
that, in elevation, is a broad-based triangle, like a gable roof, sug-
gesting that the rest of the building is below ground.

Intrigued by the troglodyte dwellings in Turkey and elsewhere.
Unlike Boullee, where there is simply the appearance of buried
architecture, these "buildings" actually are completely buried and
have no appearance from a short distance away. They can be seen as
having no foundation and as being all foundation.

In Claude-Nicolas Ledoux's "Quarters for the Rural Caretakers"
the rectangular foundation takes on a delightfully vestigial charac-
ter, as if the spherical building had evolved from it. Freed from its
supporting role, the rectangular foundation assumes an almost purely
visual function as the setting for the spherical building, which rests
on a single point.

nerary Monument (Etienne-Louis Boullee)

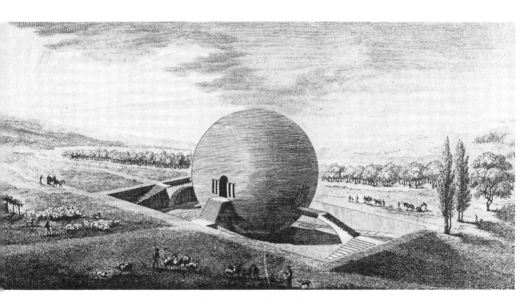

uarters for the Rural Caretakers (Claude-Nicolas Ledoux)

On the model of Burke's *artificial infinite,* I'm interested in an *ironic infinite* and an *ironic sublime.* Not a mocking, destroying irony but a positive one, like Duchamp's. What I have in mind is a sort of garden-variety sublime.

When I was teaching at Cooper Union in the first year or two of the fifties, someone told me how I could get on to the unfinished New Jersey Turnpike. I took three students and drove from somewhere in the Meadows to New Brunswick. It was a dark night and there were no lights or shoulder markers, lines, railings or anything at all except the dark pavement moving through the landscape of the flats, rimmed by hills in the distance, but punctuated by stacks, towers, fumes, and colored lights. This drive was a revealing experience. The road and much of the landscape was artificial, and yet it couldn't be called a work of art. On the other hand, it did something for me that art had never done. At first I didn't know what it was, but its effect was to liberate me from many of the views I had had about art. It seemed that there had been a reality there which had not had any expression in art.

The experience on the road was something mapped out but not socially recognized. I thought to myself, it ought to be clear that's the end of art. Most painting looks pretty pictorial after that. There is no way you can frame it, you just have to experience it. Later I discovered some abandoned airstrips in Europe—abandoned works,

Surrealist landscapes, something that had nothing to do with any function, created worlds without tradition. Artificial landscape without cultural precedent began to dawn on me. There is a drill ground in Nuremberg, large enough to accomodate two million men. The entire field is enclosed with high embankments and towers. The concrete approach is three sixteen-inch steps, one above the other, stretching for a mile or so.
Tony Smith, in an interview with Samuel Wagstaff, Jr.


The artist who is physically engulfed trys to give evidence of this experience through a limited (mapped) revision of the original unbounded state.
Smithson on the experience of boundlessness described by Ehrenzweig and Tony Smith


I had not a dispute but a disquisition with Dilke, on various subjects; several things dovetailed in my mind, & at once it struck me, what quality went to form a Man of Achievement especially in Literature & which Shakespeare possessed so enormously—I mean Negative Capability, that is when man is capable of being in uncertainties, Mysteries, doubts, without any irritable reaching after fact & reason....
John Keats, in a letter to his brothers

The growth of new images in art and new concepts in science is nourished by the conflict between two opposing principles. The analysis of abstract gestalt elements is pitted against complex scanning, fragmentation against wholeness, differentiation against dedifferentiation. Anton Ehrenzweig, *The Hidden Order of Art*

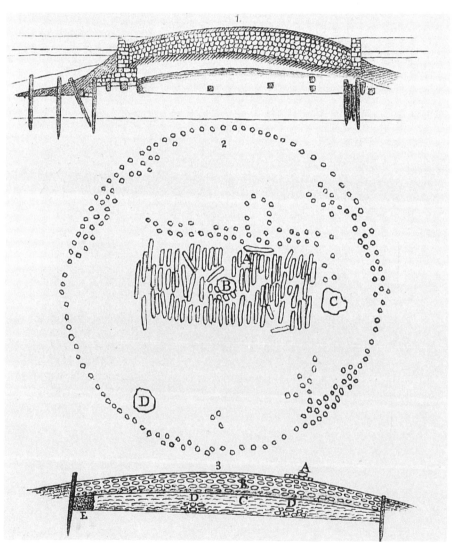

Irish Crannoges

Foundation of Seedpods on My Glove

I've been thinking about small artworks, particularly those dealing with architecture, in relation to my foundations of red and yellow leaves and *Foundation of Seedpods on My Glove*. Joel Shapiro's tiny cast iron houses from the seventies have a similar feel of condensed structure reorienting and enlarging the space around it. Though they are still and heavy, they have a whirling energy to them, as if they had just touched down, like Dorothy's house in "The Wizard of Oz." Charles Simmonds' colonies of miniature cliff dwellings and pueblos have this same quality of disorientation of time and space. The structures have the paradoxical quality of being unobtrusive and easy to overlook while demanding concentration and long observation if you are to take them in and understand their intricacies. There is a slight, offhand humor in both artists, coupled with an attention to detail, that I share.

An ecclesiastic foundation is the making over of temporal goods to an ecclesiastical corporation or individual, either by gift during life or by will after death, on the condition of some spiritual work being done either in perpetuity or for a very long time.

*The Catholic Encyclopedia*

...In that Empire, the Art of Cartography reached such Perfection that the map of one Province alone took up the whole of a City, and the map of the empire, the whole of a Province. In time, those Unconscionable Maps did not satisfy and the Colleges of Cartographers set up a map of the Empire which had the size of the empire itself and coincided with it point by point. Less Addicted to the Study of Cartography, Succeeding Generations understood that this Widespread Map was Useless and not without Impiety they abandoned it to the Inclemencies of the Sun and of the Winters. In the deserts of the West some mangled Ruins of the Map lasted on, inhabited by Animals and Beggars; in the whole Country there are no other relics of the Disciplines of Geography.

Suarez Miranda:—Viajes de Varones Prudentes,—
Book Four, Chapter XLV, 1658.

Jorge Luis Borges, "On Rigor in Science"

Walter de Maria's *Half-Mile-Long Drawing* in the Mohave Desert has the relationship to landscape I've been thinking of: minimal marking, defining and condensing interior space, drawing in and focusing exterior space, a way of organizing the landscape. Unlike my foundations, he doesn't completely enclose, giving the work much more projection into the landscape, it takes possession of more space. My work is more intimate, as is the landscape here.

Despite the distances involved in the lines at Nazca, there is something intimate and unimposing, even off-hand, about the work. The lines were constructed by a process of removal. They do not impress by indicating superhuman efforts or staggering feats of engineering. Rather it is the maker's care and economy and insight into the nature of a particular landscape that impresses.
Robert Morris, "Aligned with Nazca"

Pathway Into Infinity (Nazca Lines). Photo © 1986 Marilyn Bridges.

▲ Foundation of Mason's Line II (Kingston, NY)

▼ Foundation of Mason's Li

Foundation of Mason's Line II

▼ Foundation of Mason's Line II

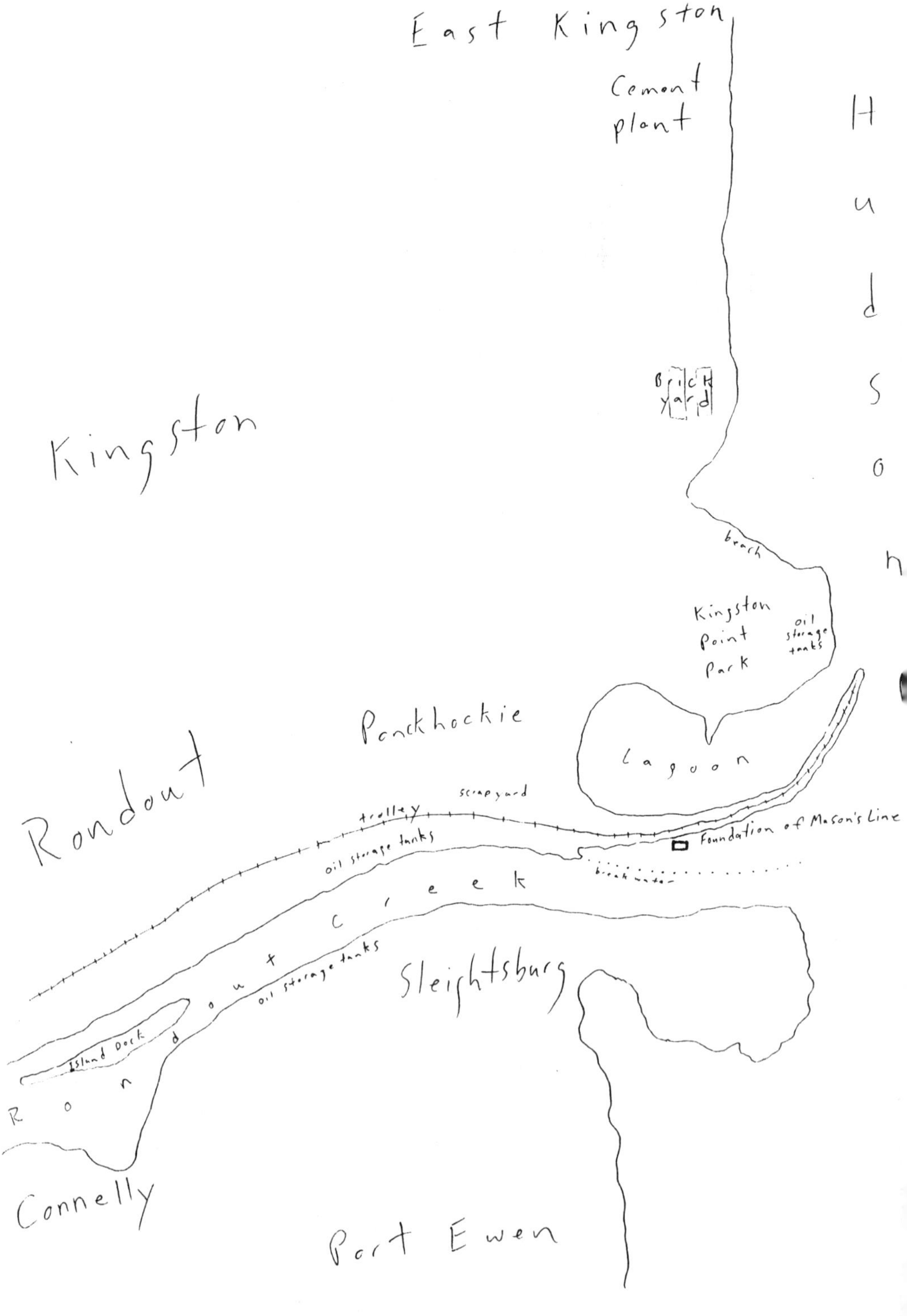

East Kingston

Cement plant

Hudson

Kingston

Brick yard

beach

Kingston Point Park

oil storage tanks

Lagoon

Panckhockie

scrapyard

Rondout

trolley

oil storage tanks

Foundation of Mason's Line

breakwater

Creek

oil storage tanks

Sleightsburg

Rondout

Island Dock

Connelly

Port Ewen

*Map 3   Foundation of Mason's Line II*

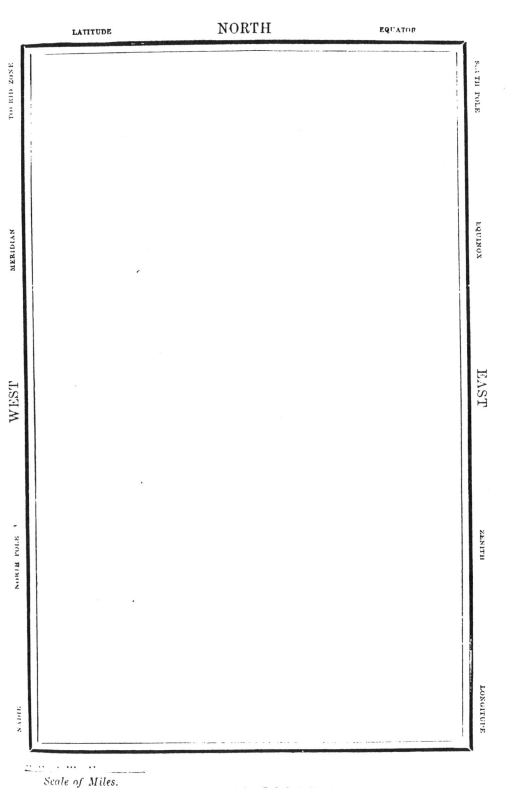

OCEAN-CHART.

m Lewis Carroll, "The Hunting of the Snark"

In a work of art any element however paltry has to be firmly related to the total structure in a complex web of cross ties radiating across the entire picture plane. There is no decisive division between the gestalt or figure and mere background elements. The complexity of any work of art however simple far outstrips the powers of conscious attention, which, with its pinpoint focus, can attend to only one thing at a time. Only the extreme undifferentiation of unconscious vision can scan these complexities. It can hold them in a single unfocused glance and treat figure and ground with equal impartiality.

Anton Ehrenzweig, *The Hidden Order of Art*


In terms of the figure/ground question, the foundation functions as a figure on the ground of the site. Like the human figure, it has a definite and immediately comprehensible shape, but it doesn't participate in the usual hierarchy of figure as active, assertively present, stated, and important, and the ground as passive, supportively present, implied, and less important. It doesn't operate like a figure in a painting or a sculpture set outside. The figure of the foundation and the ground of the site flow back and forth, defining and creating each other. The work is about the reverberations that are set up when the foundation is placed on the site, so the foundation cannot be separated from the site, from the ground.

I like the reversible male/female aspect of this figure/ground inter-action. It reminds me of Carl Andre's statement "A thing is a hole in a thing it is not," and of Duchamp's Nine Malic Molds from the *Large Glass,* where we see only the male, vaguely suggestive exterior of the mold and must imagine the female interior shape that would be used to mold the male figure. There is a movement from a represented, vaguely male form to an imagined female form to an imagined male form. I felt a similar movement when I saw Richard Artschwager's series of packing crates, where the exterior form of each crate suggests an object that it was made to protect. I looked at the lighted exterior but I thought about the darkened interior. This in turn suggests Boullee's sunken architecture, where the visible portion of the building suggests that the majority of the building is hidden from view underground.

## APPENDIX F.

### CIRCULAR PILE DWELLING IN THE LAKE OF MORAT.

Dr. Keller's opinion has always been adverse to the idea of lake dwellings having been circular. It was therefore with some surprise that on the 15th November I received from him a postcard giving me information of the discovery of a circular pile dwelling. It would be highly desirable if all scientific men were as candid as he is. The very last item in his valuable work seems to go contrary to one of his long-cherished ideas, but he at once communicates the information : facts and facts only form the platform of science. As his letter on the postcard contains only two or three lines, it is here copied verbatim :—

' A circular pile dwelling on a small island, at Fang, in the lake of Morat.

FIG. 50.

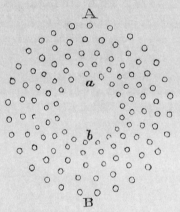

' From A to B is 44 yards.

' From $a$ to $b$, $7\frac{1}{2}$ yards.

' The rings of piles are about a yard apart. The piles consist of split oak.—Zürich, 12 Nov. 1877.—F. K.'

Foundation of removed tiles. Could also be done outside from re-moved cobblestones, bricks, etc. Or of removed sod, both space with sod removed and removed sod laid out in another space, maybe close by so they can be viewed simultaneously.

In Andre's "rugs" it's as if the mass has been squeezed away. In my pieces it's as if it has been blown away or washed away, a lighter feeling. Both are physically more or less two dimensional but take possession of the space around and above them.

Foundation of punctuation

single mark—comma, exclamation, etc.—and mixed

Our usual method of defining the foundations is to trace out several lines, known as baselines, in the following manner. From a mid-point at the front, we extend a line right to the back of the work; halfway along it we fix a stake into the ground, and through this, following the rules of geometry, we extend the perpendicular. We then relate all the measurements to these two lines. This works wonderfully in every way: the parallel lines are easily drawn, the angles can be defined accurately, and the parts conform and corre-spond exactly to one another.
Leone Battista Alberti, *On the Art of Building in Ten Books*

One might say a *de-architecturing* takes place before the artist sets his limits outside the studio or the room.

Robert Smithson, "A Sedimentation of the Mind"

In these terms, my foundations are the beginning of a *re-architecturing*, a return to limits and enclosure by placing the foundation form in the landscape.

*Rectangular Figure (Hoario Terme)*, a Bronze Age rock drawing from Valcamonica, Italy

Then within this substructure lay a second foundation, far enough inside the first to leave ample room for cohorts in line of battle to take position on the broad top of the rampart for its defense. Having laid these two foundations at this distance from one another, build cross walls between them, uniting the outer and inner foundation, in a comb-like arrangement, set like the teeth of a saw. With this form of construction, the enormous burden of earth will be distributed into small bodies, and will not lie with all its weight in one crushing mass so as to thrust out the superstructures.

Vitruvius, *The Ten Books of Architecture*

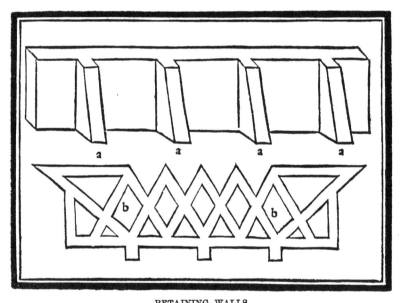

RETAINING WALLS
(From the edition of Vitruvius by Fra Giocondo, Venice 1511)

I was thinking last night on the bridge about my propensity for building foundations I can look down onto. Does this pull me and the viewer away from the active participation in the work that I want?

Smithson addresses this in "...The Earth, Subject to Cruel Cataclysms, Is a Cruel Master," saying that a work viewed from above doesn't become an object. "What you have there are many different scale changes...close, medium and long views. Scale becomes a matter of interchangeable distances."

I want the feel of being in the foundation, in its space, but I also want the long view of it as an image, complete. And the view down is still a space relation, only a different one.

Perhaps the most compelling aspect of Minimalism was that it was the only art of objects (aside from architecture) which ever attempted to mediate between the notational knowledge of flat concerns (systems, the diagrammatic, the logically constructed and placed, the preconceived) and the concerns of objects (the relativity of perception in depth).
Robert Morris, "Aligned with Nazca"

This is the place where the foundations come together with the Nazca lines, de Maria's *Half-Mile-Long Drawing,* and Richard Artschwager's *blps,* in terms of marking space and your place in it. This use of marking brings painting and drawing concerns into space, into three dimensions.

In short, Diderot held that the poetics or imaginative essence of depictions of ruins required that the beholder be compelled to enter the painting, to meditate not only on but among the remains of ancient civilizations.

...

Accordingly, Diderot seems to have held that an essential object of paintings belonging to those genres [the lesser genres of pastoral scenes, landscapes with figures, depictions of ruins, still lifes] was to induce in the beholder a particular psycho-physical condition, equivalent in kind and intensity to a profound experience of nature, which for the sake of brevity might be characterized as one of existential reverie or *repos delicieux*. In that state of mind and body a wholly passive receptivity becomes the vehicle of an apprehension of the fundamental beneficence of the natural world; the subject's awareness of the passage of time and, on occasion, of his very surroundings may be abolished; and he comes to experience a pure and intense sensation of the sweetness and as it were the self-sufficiency of his own existence.

Michael Fried, *Absorption and Theatricality*


FOUNDATIONS

*Deut.* 32. 22. and set on fire the *f.* of the mountains
*Ezra* 4. 12. have set up the walls and joined the *f.*
*Job* 38.4. where wast thou when I laid the *f.* of earth
    6. whereupon are the *f.* thereof fastened
*Prov.* 54. 11. I will lay thy *f.* with sapphires
*Jer.* 50. 15. her *f.* are fallen, her walls are thrown down
    51. 26. they shall not take of thee a stone for *f.*
*Lam.* 4. 11. and it hast devoured the *f.* thereof
*Ezek.* 41. 8. the *f.* of the side chambers were a full reed
*Heb.* 11. 10. for he looked for a city that hath *f.*
*Rev.* 21. 14. the walls of the city had twelve *f.*
    19. the *f.* were garnished with precious stones

*A Complete Concordance to the Holy Scriptures of the Old and New Testaments,* Alexander Cruden, compiler

Foundation of Sumac I, *left;* Foundation of Sumac II, *right* ▶

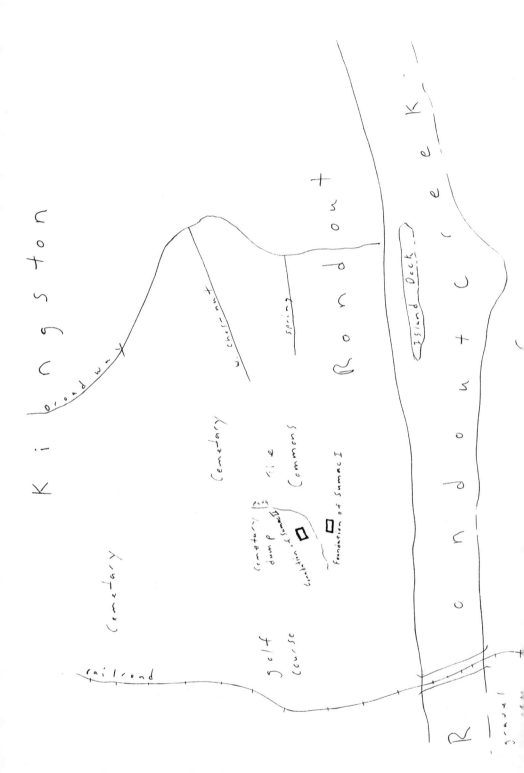

*Map 4   Foundations of Sumac I and II*

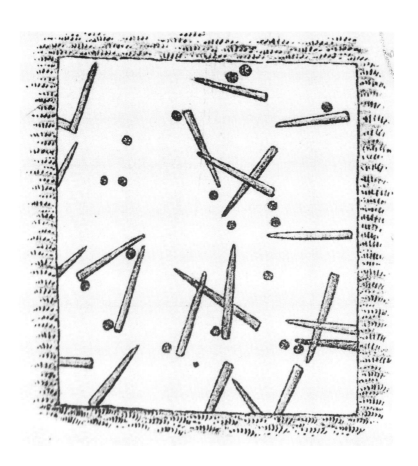

The foundations are interventions into nature, cuts into its space, like Matta-Clark's cuts into buildings. As cuts go, they are more scratch than wound.

The foundations can be seen as shelters and containers for the self as a whole and for all the things—emotions, fluids, thoughts—that are enclosed in the body. They are also self-portraits—reflections or surrogates or versions of the self, images of my presence at the site. This suggests a relationship between my photographs and the "me at monument" genre of tourist snapshots: me at the Eiffel Tower, me at the Pyramids, me at the Taj Mahal. The twist is that the foundation is both a natural product (a body) and an artificial product (a building), and so the photographs are part of a sub-genre, "me *as* monument."

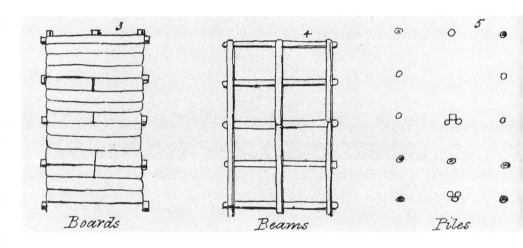

Boards          Beams          Piles

Many of the monuments, such as those to the famous bishop and captain Absalon and to the astronomer Tycho Brahe, were examples of *architecture parlante,* the forms and decorative elements reflecting the essential nature of the person's virtues and accomplishments. Richard Etlin, *The Architecture of Death*

Barrytown Foundations (Annandale, NY)

▼ Barrytown Foundations (detail)

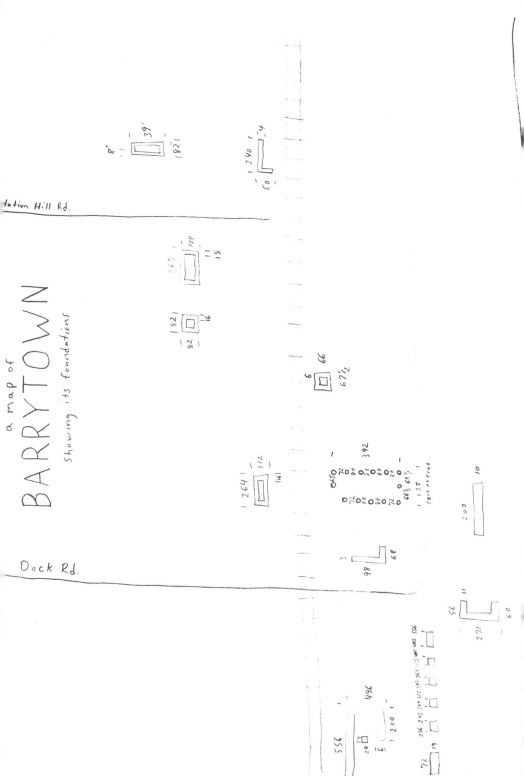

# AN

# ENCYCLOPÆDIA OF ANTIQUITIES;

AND

## ELEMENTS OF ARCHÆOLOGY.

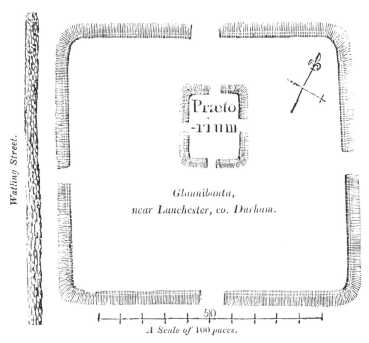

Glannibanta,
near Lanchester, co. Durham.

*A Scale of* 100 *paces.*

*A square Roman Camp, the* CONSULAR *Form, according to Lipsius.* See p. 558.

## CHAPTER XI.

*Earthworks—Fortresses—Rude Stoneworks.*

AMBERLEY—AMBURY. Mr. Gough says, that the first term denoted any earthworks, and a Danish camp on Minchinhampton Common is so called; but *Ambury* is applied to an old Druid temple near Huddersfield, co. York.[a]

The etymon of the first syllable is uncertain.

BARROWS. In that valuable and truly national Work, "The Sepulchral Monuments of Great Britain," Mr. Gough observes, that BARROWS are the most ancient monuments in the world. They were both tombs and altars. For the

---

[a] Higgins's Druids, 232.

# Birds eye view of the Platform.
## Scale – 1/70.

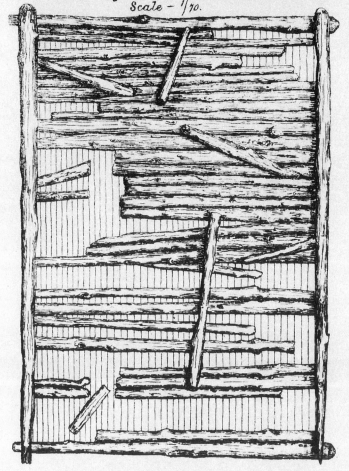

## PLAN.

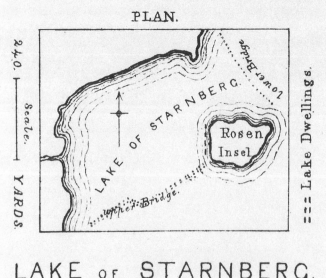

240.

Scale.

YARDS.

LAKE OF STARNBERG.

Rosen Insel.

Lower Bridge.

Upper Bridge.

::: Lake Dwellings.

# LAKE OF STARNBERG.
## Rosen Insel.

As regards the construction of footings (that is to say, the section bringing the foundations up to the level of the area), I find that the ancients offer no advice on the matter, except, as we mentioned above, that any stone showing defects after two years in the open should be consigned to the foundations. As in the army, where lazy and cowardly soldiers, incapable of enduring sun and dust, are sent back home, not without a measure of disgrace, so too, soft or enervated stone is relegated to the depths to continue its idle ways in shameful darkness. In spite of this, I read in some historical works that the ancients would devote their every care and attention to constructing the underground footings, so that, as far as possible, they would be every bit as solid as the rest of the wall.
Leone Battista Alberti, *The Art of Building in Ten Books*


A beautiful foundation for a boathouse on the east shore of the Hudson, just south of the gravel quarry after leaving Poughkeepsie. I've had many one- or two-second glimpses of it from the train, particularly in winter when the view is unobstructed. It is built of stone, bluestone most likely, and extends about thirty feet along the shore, twenty feet out from it, with a ten foot opening to the river. Even when the river is choppy, the water inside the foundation is very calm.

# Bibliography

Alberti, Leone Battista. *On the Art of Building in Ten Books*. Translated by Joseph Rykert, Neal Leach and Robert Taverner. Cambridge: MIT Press, 1988.

Bachelard, Gaston. *The Poetics of Space*. Translated by Maria Jolas. 1964; Boston: Beacon Press, 1994.

Borges, Jorge Luis. "On Rigor in Science" in *Dreamtigers*. Translated by Mildred Boyer and Harold Morland. Introduction by Miguel Enguídanos. "The Texas Pan-American Series." Austin: University of Texas Press, 1964.

Buttrick, George A., ed. *The Interpreter's Dictionary of the Bible*. 4 vols. New York: Abingdon Press, 1962.

Carroll, Lewis. *The Hunting of the Snark: An Agony in Eight Fits*. London: MacMillan, 1876.

*The Catholic Encyclopedia: An International Work of Reference on the Constitution, Doctrine, Discipline, and History of the Catholic Church*. Charles G. Herbermann et. al., editors. 15 vols. New York: Robert Appleton Company, 1909.

Cayeux, Jean de. *Hubert Robert et les jardins*. Paris: Herscher, 1987.

Cruden, Alexander, compiler. *A Complete Concordance to the Holy Scriptures of the Old and New Testaments*. New York: Fleming H. Revell Company, 1984.

Burke, Edmund. *A Philosophical Enquiry into the Origin of Our Ideas of the Sublime and Beautiful*. Edited and with an introduction by James T. Boulton. Notre Dame: University of Notre Dame Press, 1958.

Downing, Andrew Jackson. *Landscape Gardening and Rural Architecture*. 1865; New York: Dover Publications, 1991.

Ehrenzweig, Anton. *The Hidden Order of Art: A Study in the Psychology of Artistic Imagination*. Berkeley: University of California Press, 1967.

Etlin, Richard A. *The Architecture of Death: The Transformation of the Cemetary in Eighteenth-Century Paris*. Cambridge, MIT Press, 1984.

Fosbroke, Thomas Dudley. *An Encyclopedia of Antiquities and Elements of Archeology Classical and Mediaeval*. 2 vols. London: M.A. Nattali, 1843.

Fried, Michael. *Absorption and Theatricality: Painting and Beholder in the Age of Diderot*. Berkeley: University of California Press, 1980.

Harper, Prudence Oliver. *Assyrian Origins: Discoveries at Ashur on the Tigris*. New York: Metropolitan Museum of Art, 1995.

Keats, John. *The Selected Letters of John Keats*. Edited and with an introduction by Lionel Trilling. New York: Farrar, Straus and Young, 1951.

Keller, Ferdinand. *The Lake Dwellings of Switzerland and Other Parts of Europe*. London: Longmans, Green, and Co, 1878.

Krauss, Rosalind, "Sculpture in the Expanded Field," *October* 8, Spring 1979.

Lemagny, Jean-Claude. *Visionary Architects: Boullee, Ledoux, Lequeu*. Houston: University of St. Thomas, 1968.

Mellaart, James, *Çatal Hüyük: A Neolithic Town in Anatolia*. 1967; New York: McGraw Hill Book Co., 1987.

Morris, Robert. "Aligned with Nazca." *Artforum*, October 1975, pp. 26-39.

Paturi, Felix, R. *Prehistoric Heritage*. Translated by Tania and Bernard Alexander. New York: Charles Scribner's Sons, 1979.

*Random House Dictionary of the English Language*. Jess Stein et al., editors. Random House, NY, 1971.

Smith, Tony. "Talking with Tony Smith," *Artforum*, December 1966, pp. 14-19 [Tony Smith interviewed by Samuel Wagstaff, Jr.].

Smithson, Robert. *The Collected Writings*. Edited by Jack Flam. "Documents of Twentieth Century Art." Berkeley: University of California Press, 1996.

Wakefield, David. *French Eighteenth-Century Painting*. New York: Alpine Fine Arts Collection, 1984.

Vidler, Anthony. *Claude-Nicolas Ledoux: Architecture and Social Reform at the End of the Ancien Régime*. Cambridge: MIT Press, 1990.

Vitruvius Pollio, Marcus. *The Ten Books of Architecture*. Translated by Morris Hicky Morgan. New York: 1914; Dover Publications, 1960.

James Walsh is a sculptor living in Brooklyn, New York. Born in 1961, he studied English at Hobart and William Smith Colleges and Oxford University, began doing visual work in 1986, and has recently been producing sculptures that recreate architectural elements, such as awnings, fences, and railings. He has had numerous solo and group shows, and has received a Fulbright Fellowship for 1997–98 to work in Istanbul.